T0380937

Mankind

Holy Quran
Chapter (114) Workbook

Visit our website at:
Quranworkbook.com

Fadwa Amin Zagzoug

To order additional copies of this book, contact:
Xlibris
844-714-8691
www.Xlibris.com
Orders@Xlibris.com

ISBN: Softcover   979-8-3694-2283-0
          EBook   979-8-3694-2287-8

Library of Congress Control Number: 2024910299

Print information available on the last page

Rev. date: 01/24/2025

Contents

- **Introduction**

  I.   Acknowledgements... 2

  II. How to Use this Workbook Chart.................................. 3

  III. Quran Chapter 114 Summary..................................... 4

  IV. Surat An-Nas full page 5

- **Vocabulary worksheets**

  I.   Section One- letters to words (Verses 1 through 6) 7

  Designed for beginners who do not know the Arabic alphabet or need a review!

  II. Section Two- words to verses (Verses 1 through 6)................................. 37

  Designed for learners who already know the Arabic alphabet letters.

- **Reflection worksheets.. 49**

  Medium to high level reflection exercises. Introduction to the verses' concept, reflection and expansion on the meanings. Connecting verses to other Quranic verses and/or Hadith Sahih. Exploration of real-life applications and personal lessons.

- **Quiz Review Exercises....................................... 69**

  Vocabulary review for the Surah, assessment, and mastery activities. Word search, matching, copying complete surah, and crossword puzzle.

- **Surat An-Nas Board Game Challenge**

  I.   Game Rules... 79

  II. Board 80

  III. Board Game Questions 82

Acknowledgments

I am forever thankful and grateful towards my one and only Creator, Allah (الله) ﷻ . I am thankful that Allah ﷻ inspired me to have this quality to begin with.

I am also thankful for all God's prophets and messengers (الأنبياء والرُسُل) especially the last Prophet, The Prophet of Islam, Muhammad, peace and blessings be upon him ﷺ .

(رسول الله محمد بن عبد الله صلى الله عليه وسلم تسليما كثيراً)

Prophets and messengers passed knowledge to us from God and have endured great hardship in their path. They are our role models and for them I am forever thankful and grateful.

Abu Huraira reported: Prophet Muhammad ﷺ , said:

" Whoever does not thank people has not thanked Allah."

عَن أَبي هُريرة رضي الله عنه قال: قال رسول الله صلى الله عليه وسَلَّم: " من لا يَشكُر الناس لا يَشكُر الله "

حَديث صَحيح- سُنن الترمذي .

All through my life, God Almighty put people in my path that are kind, knowledgeable, giving, and sometimes of deep faith. The first people that come to mind are my parents, husband, grandparents, family, and friends. My teachers are one of my greatest blessings as well since they always inspired me to do my best and dealt with my short comings with great patience and love. I also extend my special thanks and gratitude to Shaykha Ebtsam Fawzy who reviewed this workbook for accuracy and correctness. Shaykha Ebtsam is a Hafiza of the Holy Quran and holds an Ijazah in the Qira'a of Asem. She is also certified in memorizing the Holy Quran with Hafs narration from Al-Sunnah AL Muhammadiyah institute cooperated with al-Azhar. Shaykha Ebtsam is currently teaching online classes through Jannat Al Quran website (https://www.jannatalquran.com). Her experience with teaching Quran to non-Arabic native speakers has made this workbook a valuable resource to both learners and teachers of the Holy Quran. In addition, my special thanks go to Nesma Abdelrahman for the wonderful graphic design she did on this workbook. I really appreciate her patience and the hard work she did to make the workbook look so professional and appealing to the reader.

How to use this workbook?
(Summary Chart)

Step 1
Listen
to the verses recited by a professional (Example: Mahmoud Al-Hussary recitation)

Step 2
Learn meaning
by reading English translation (Example: QuranEnc.com)

Step 3
Do worksheets
one verse at a time

Step 4
Recite
verses from workbook or from memory

Step 5
Repeat
with a new verse until entire surah is complete

Step 6
Play
the board game to review the entire surah

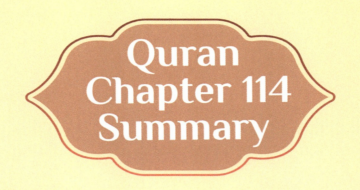

Quran Chapter 114 Summary

مُلَخَّص سُورَة النَّاس

Allah ﷻ loves us so dearly that in this last surah of the Holy Quran He gives us an opportunity of protection and refuge from the most hideous evil of all- the whisper of Satan and evil mankind.

Allah's doors are always open to call on Him for protection, guidance, and sustenance.
All we have to do is to believe in Him as our only Lord, King, and God.
He teaches us in this Surah to say: I seek refuge in You my Lord, my King, and my God from the evil of the retreating whisperer.

In The Name Of Allah
the Most Gracious, the Most Merciful

﴿ قُلْ أَعُوذُ بِرَبِّ ٱلنَّاسِ (1) مَلِكِ ٱلنَّاسِ (2) إِلَهِ ٱلنَّاسِ (3) مِن شَرِّ ٱلْوَسْوَاسِ ٱلْخَنَّاسِ (4) ٱلَّذِى يُوَسْوِسُ فِى صُدُورِ ٱلنَّاسِ (5) مِنَ ٱلْجِنَّةِ وَٱلنَّاسِ (6) ﴾

" Say, "I seek refuge with the Lord of mankind (1) The King of mankind (2) The God of mankind (3) From the evil of the retreating whisperer (4) Who whispers into the breasts of mankind (5) From among jinn and mankind (6) "

سورَةُ النّاسِ
Surat An-Nas

Chapter 114

Vocabulary Worksheets

Section 1
(Letters to Words)

l. Trace

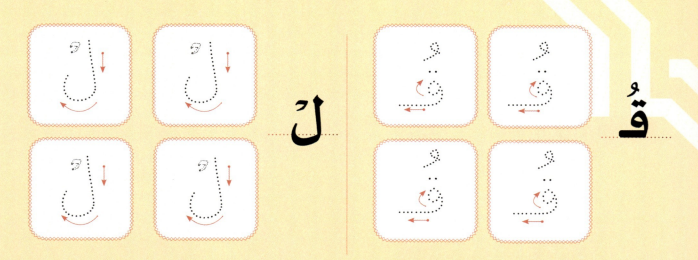

ل

قُ

ll. Color & then copy

(Say) ــــــ قُلْ ـــــ

ــــــــــــ 2	ــــــــــــ 1
ــــــــــــ 4	ــــــــــــ 3
ــــــــــــ 6	ــــــــــــ 5

l. Trace

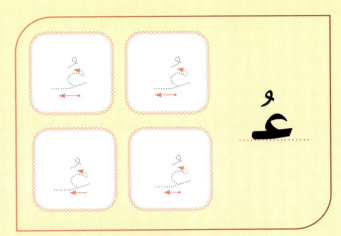

عُ

أَ

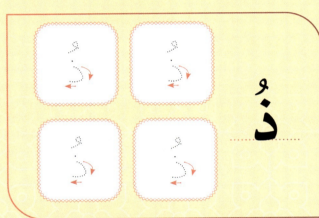

ذُ

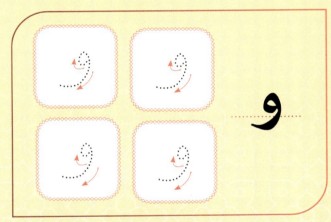

و

ll. Color & then copy

أَعُوذُ

(l Seek refuge)

4 _____	1 _____
5 _____	2 _____
6 _____	3 _____

l. Trace

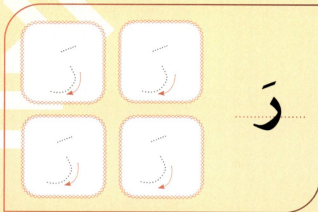

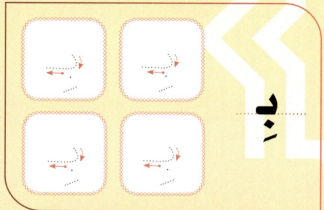

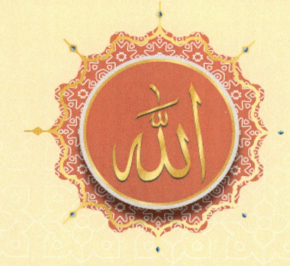

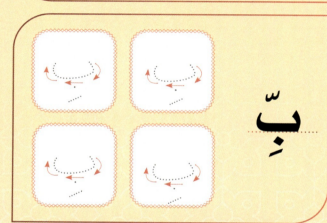

ll. Color & then copy

بِرَبّ

(with the Lord of)

lll. Who is our Lord ?

_____

5	_____ 3	_____ 1
_____ 6	_____ 4	_____ 2

l. Trace

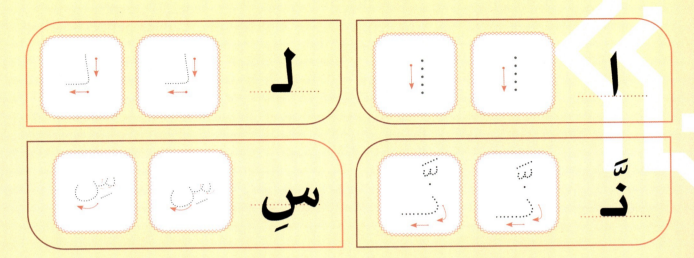

ا

لَ

نَ

سِ

ll. Color & then copy

ٱلنَّاسِ

(mankind) _____

_____ 5	_____ 3	_____ 1
_____ 6	_____ 4	_____ 2

lll. Who are mankind?

Answer:
All humans: Muslim & non-Muslim, black&
white, old & young, male &female, rich
& poor, sick & healthy, etc.

l. Connect the Arabic letters to make the words for verse number one.
(Letters are scrambled)

(mouth image)	---------------------------- 1	لْ . قُ
(man image)	---------------------------- 2	ذُ . و . عُ . أَ
(Allah image)	---------------------------- 3	بّ . بِ . رَ
(people image)	---------------------------- 4	لـ . ا . سِ . آ . نَّ

Directions: Match the word to the correct picture.

قُلْ

أَعُوذُ

بِرَبِّ

ٱلنَّاسِ

4. Write English Translation	3. Copy	2. Copy	1. Trace
....	....	....	قُلْ
....	....	....	أَعُوذُ
....	....	....	بِرَبِّ
....	....	....	النَّاسِ

5. Copy the complete verse below four times

....1

....2

....3

....4

Mankind

l. Trace

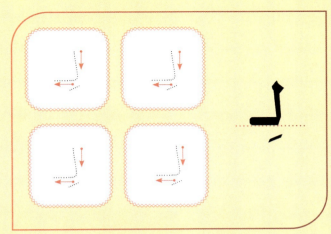

لِ

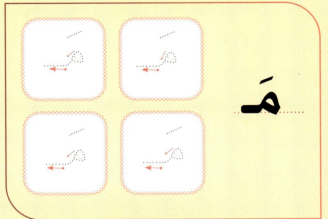

مَ

كِ

اللّٰه

ll. Color & then copy

مَلِك

(The King)

lll. Who is the King of all kings?

_____

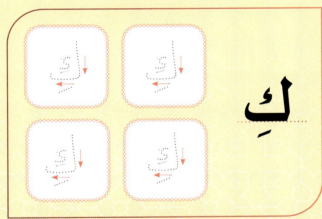

_____ 5	_____ 3	_____ 1
_____ 6	_____ 4	_____ 2

l. Connect the Arabic letters to make the words for verse number two.
(Letters are scrambled)

	_____ 1	لِ . ـكِ . مَ
	_____ 2	لـ . آ . سِ . ا . نَّ

Directions: Match the word to the correct picture.

 مَلِك

 آلنَّاسِ

Verse number (2) worksheet (C)

4. Write English Translation	3. Copy	2. Copy	1. Trace
....	....	....	مَلِكِ
....	....	....	النَّاسِ

5. Copy the complete verse below four times

1
2
3
4

l. Trace

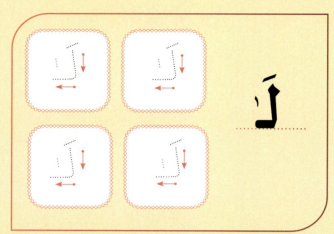

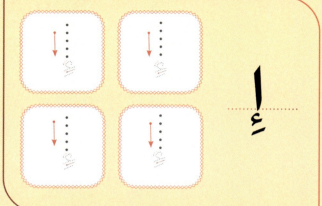

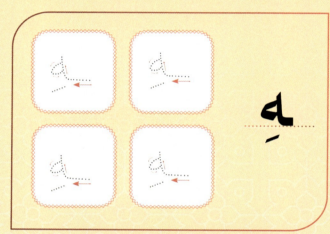

ll. Color & then copy

(The God)

lll. Who is our God?

5

3

1

6

4

2

l. Connect the Arabic letters to make the words for verse number three.
(Letters are scrambled)

	ـــــــــــــــــــــــــــــ 1	لَ . إِ . هِ
	ـــــــــــــــــــــــــــــ 2	نَّ . آ . سِ . ١ . لـ

Directions: Match the word to the correct picture.

إِلَـهِ

ٱلنَّاسِ

4. Write English Translation	3. Copy	2. Copy	1. Trace
....	....	....	اِلـٰهِ
....	....	....	النَّاسِ

5. Copy the complete verse below four times

1. ....
2. ....
3. ....
4. ....

1. Trace

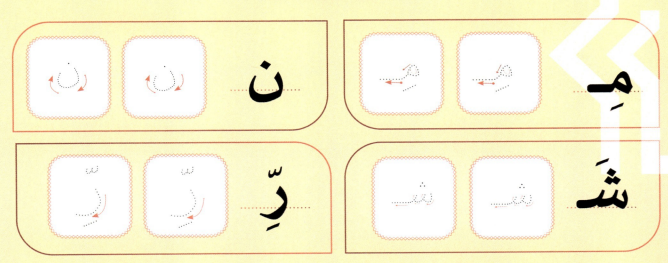

ن

مِ

رِّ

شَ

II. Color & then copy

مِن شَرِّ

(from the evil of)

_____ 5	_____ 3	_____ 1
_____ 6	_____ 4	_____ 2

III. What should we say to protect ourselves from evil:

أَعُوذُ بِاللَّه

Answer:

I seek refuge in Allah

أَعُوذُ بِاللَّه

I. Trace

ا

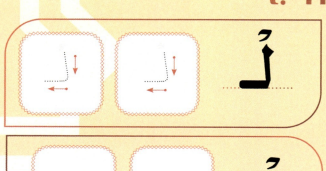

لُ

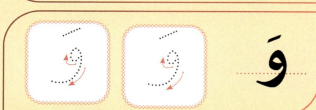

وَ

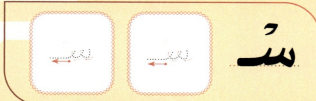

سُ

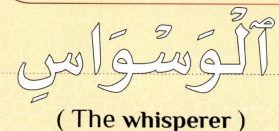

سِ

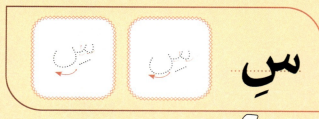

ٱلْوَسْوَاسِ

(The **whisperer**)

II. Color & then copy

_____ 5	_____ 3	_____ 1
_____ 6	_____ 4	_____ 2

III. Who is the evil whisperer?

Answer:

Satan and evil mankind.

l. Trace

اُ

ا

نَّ

خَ

سِ

ll. Color & then copy

الْخَنَّاسِ

(The retreating)

_____ 5	_____ 3	_____ 1
_____ 6	_____ 4	_____ 2

lll. a) Who keeps the evil whisperer away?

Answer:

Our Lord, our King, and our God **ALLAH**ﷻ

b) True/False: The evil whisperer never gives up.

l. Connect the Arabic letters to make the words for verse number four.
(Letters are scrambled)

From	------------------------------- 1	ن . مِ
Evil	------------------------------- 2	رِّ . شَ
The Whisperer	------------------------------- 3	لُّ . سُ . آ . سِ . وَ . وَ . ا
The Retreating	------------------------------- 4	نَّ . آ . سِ . ا . لُّ . خَ

4. Write English Translation	3. Copy	2. Copy	1. Trace
....	....	....	مِن شَرِّ
....	....	....	الْوَسْوَاسِ
....	....	....	الْخَنَّاسِ

5. Copy the complete verse below four times

....	1
....	2
....	3
....	4

l. Trace

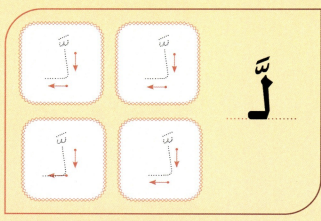

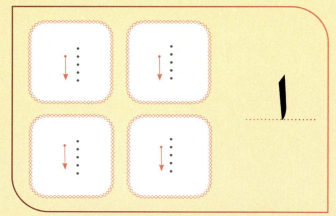

l. Color & then copy

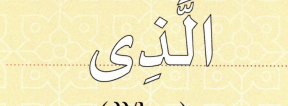

(Who)

l. Trace

l. Color & then copy

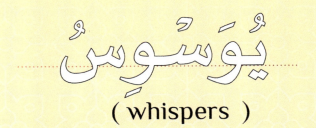

(whispers)

------------------------- 5	------------------------- 3	------------------------- 1
------------------------- 6	------------------------- 4	------------------------- 2

l. Trace

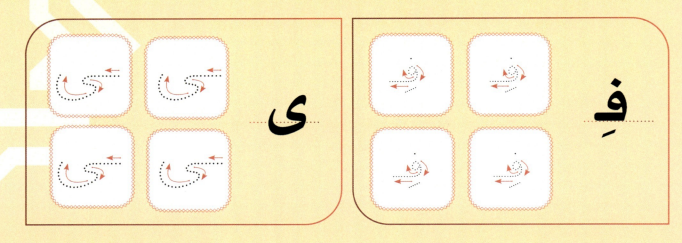

ll. Color & then copy

فِي

(in)

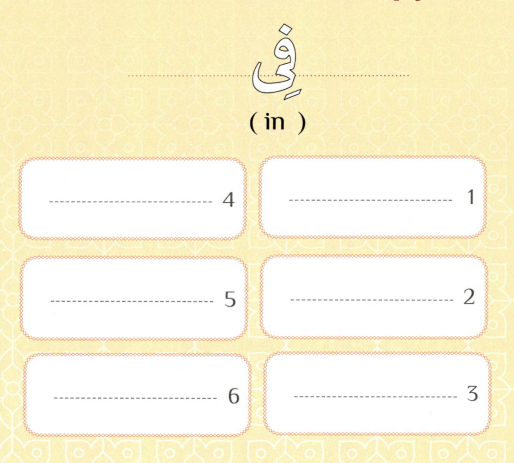

l. Trace

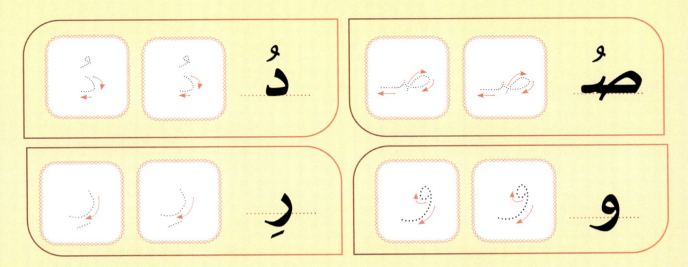

ll. Color & then copy

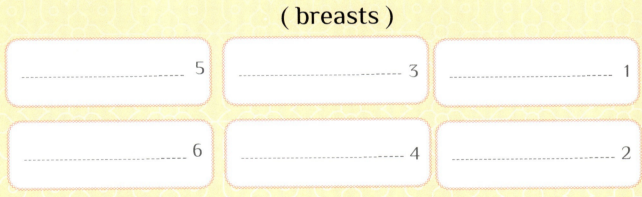

(breasts)

------------------- 5	------------------- 3	------------------- 1
------------------- 6	------------------- 4	------------------- 2

lll. **a)** Is this word plural or singular?

b) What is the singular of

صُدُورٍ in Arabic?

Answer:

صَدْر

l. Connect the Arabic letters to make the words for verse number five.
(Letters are scrambled)

Who	1 -------------------		ذِ.ى.ا.لَّ
	2 -------------------		يُ.وِ.سُ.سُ.وَ
ln	3 -------------------		ى.فِ
	4 -------------------		و.صُ.رِ.دُ
	5 -------------------		سِ.آ.ا.لـ.نَّ

4. Write English Translation	3. Copy	2. Copy	1. Trace
....	....	....	ٱلَّذِى
....	....	....	يُوَسْوِسُ
....	....	....	فِى
....	....	....	صُدُورِ
....	....	....	ٱلنَّاسِ

l. Trace

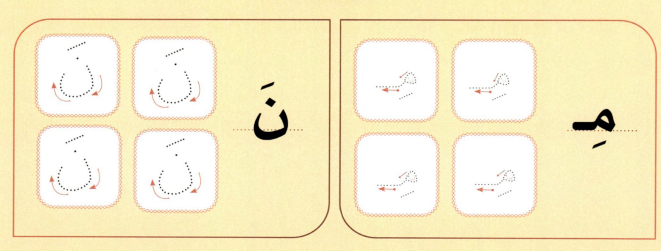

ll. Color & then copy

(from)

I. Trace

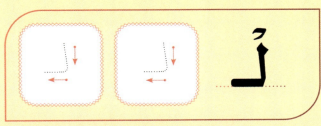

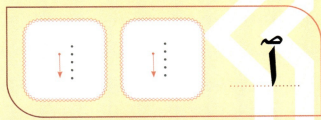

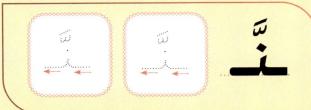

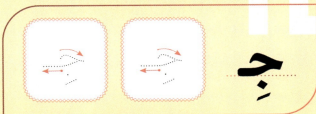

II. Color & then copy

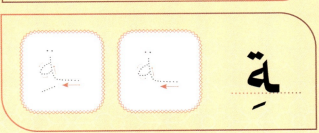

(jinn)

| _____ 5 | _____ 3 | _____ 1 |
| _____ 6 | _____ 4 | _____ 2 |

III. a) What are jinn created from?

> **Answer:**
> A smokeless flame of fire.

b) True/False: ALL jinn are disbelievers.

l. Connect the Arabic letters to make the words for verse number six.
(Letters are scrambled)

From Among	1 -----------	نَ . مِ
jinn	2 -----------	جِ . لُ . ةِ . آ . نَّ
	3 -----------	ا . نَّ . سِ . آ . لـ

ll. Directions: Match the word to the correct picture.

jinn

الْجِنَّةِ

النَّاسِ

Verse number (6) worksheet (D)

4. Write English Translation	3. Copy	2. Copy	1. Trace
....	....	....	مِنْ
....	....	....	الْجِنَّةِ
....	....	....	وَالنَّاسِ

II. Copy the complete verse below four times

1 ....
2 ....
3 ....
4 ....

سورَةُ النَّاسِ
Surat An-Nas

Chapter 114

Vocabulary Worksheets

Section 2
(Words to Verses)

I. **Unscramble** the following words from verse one
and then **copy** the complete verse
five times on the lines provided below.

بِرَبِّ / أَعُوذُ / قُلْ / ٱلنَّاسِ

Say, "I seek refuge with the Lord of mankind

....1

....2

....3

....4

....5

II. **Answer the following questions:**

1. **Who is this verse speaking to?**

....

2. **What are we seeking refuge from?**

....

Circle the correct meaning of each word from verse one

1

mankind	I seek refuge
with the Lord of	Say

2

mankind	I seek refuge
with the Lord of	Say

3

mankind	I seek refuge
with the Lord of	Say

4

mankind	I seek refuge
with the Lord of	Say

I. Color and Copy

النَّاسِ
(of mankind)

مَلِكِ
(The King or Sovereign)

..............1

..............1

..............2

..............2

..............3

..............3

..............4

..............4

II. Answer the following questions:

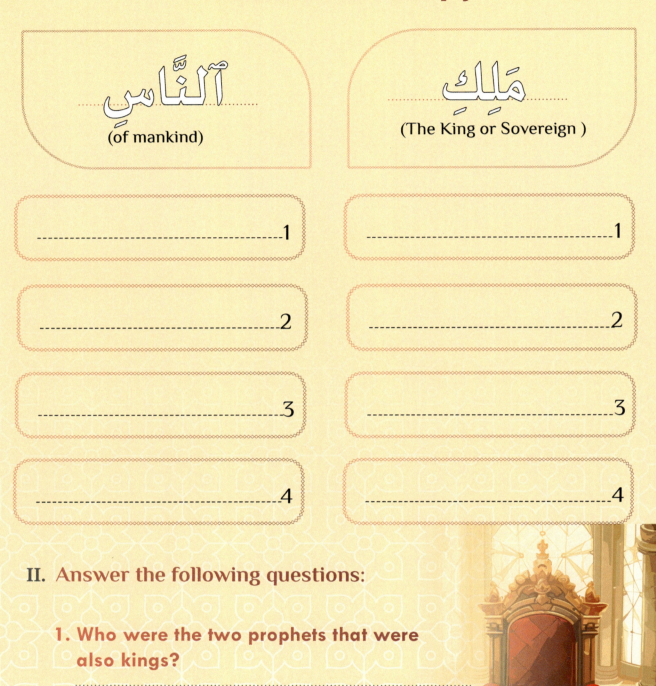

1. Who were the two prophets that were also kings?

....

2. What is the name of the Queen that lived around that time?

....

3. Do ALL mankind live in a kingdom?

....

I. Color and Copy

آلنَّاسِ
(of mankind)

إِلَهِ
(The God)

---------1

---------1

---------2

---------2

---------3

---------3

--------- 4

--------- 4

II. Answer the following questions:

1. Give some examples of acts of worship that Muslims perform.

....

2. Who taught us these acts of worship?

....

3. Who is our role model when it comes to acts of worship?

....

4. How do you know?

....

I. **Unscramble** the following words from verse 4
and then **copy** the complete verse
five times on the lines provided below.

ٱلْوَسْوَاسِ / شَرِّ / ٱلْخَنَّاسِ / مِن

From the evil of the retreating whisperer

.... 1

.... 2

.... 3

.... 4

.... 5

II. **Answer the following questions:**

1. Which vocabulary word above means (evil) ?

....

2. What does الْخَنَّاسِ mean?

....

Circle the correct meaning of each word from verse 4

| 1 | مِن | the retreating | the evil of |
| | | the whisperer | from |

| 2 | شَرِّ | the retreating | the evil of |
| | | the whisperer | from |

| 3 | ٱلْوَسْوَاسِ | the retreating | the evil of |
| | | the whisperer | from |

| 4 | ٱلْخَنَّاسِ | the retreating | the evil of |
| | | the whisperer | from |

Color and Copy

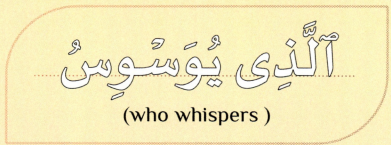

ٱلَّذِى يُوَسْوِسُ

(who whispers)

---------------------------------3

---1

---------------------------4

-----------------------------2

فِى

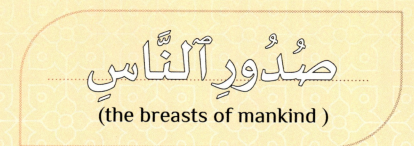

صُدُورِ ٱلنَّاسِ

(the breasts of mankind)

------------------------------------1

------------------------------------2

------------------------------------3

I. Unscramble the following words from verse 5
and then **copy** the complete verse
five times on the lines provided below.

يُوَسْوِسُ / فِ / ٱلَّذِى / صُدُورِ / ٱلنَّاسِ

Who whispers into the breasts of mankind

.... 1

.... 2

.... 3

.... 4

.... 5

II. Answer the following questions:

1. Which vocabulary word above means (breasts) ?

....

2. What does يُوَسْوِسُ **mean?**

....

I. Color and Copy

مِنَ ٱلْجِنَّةِ وَٱلنَّاسِ

-- 1

-- 2

-- 3

-- 4

II. Write down the English translation below

Section Two Key

▬ **Verse number (1) worksheet (A)**

I. قُلْ أَعُوذُ بِرَبِّ ٱلنَّاسِ

II.1. Prophet Muhammad ﷺ and all the believers.

2. The evil of the retreating whisperer.

▬ **Verse number (1) worksheet (B)**

1. Say,
2. I seek refuge
3. With the Lord of
4. Mankind

▬ **Verse number (2) worksheet**

II.1. King David داود ﷺ and also his son King Solomon سليمان ﷺ
We can read about this in Surat an-Naml النَّمل (27:15-16)

> وَلَقَدْ ءَاتَيْنَا دَاوُدَ وَسُلَيْمَٰنَ عِلْمًا وَقَالَا ٱلْحَمْدُ لِلَّهِ ٱلَّذِي فَضَّلَنَا عَلَىٰ كَثِيرٍ مِّنْ عِبَادِهِ ٱلْمُؤْمِنِينَ ﴿15﴾ وَوَرِثَ سُلَيْمَٰنُ دَاوُدَ وَقَالَ يَٰٓأَيُّهَا ٱلنَّاسُ عُلِّمْنَا مَنطِقَ ٱلطَّيْرِ وَأُوتِينَا مِن كُلِّ شَيْءٍ إِنَّ هَٰذَا لَهُوَ ٱلْفَضْلُ ٱلْمُبِينُ ﴿16﴾
>
> " And we gave David and Solomon knowledge, and they said, "All praise be to Allah, Who has favored us over many of His believing slaves ﴿15﴾ Solomon succeeded David, and said, "O people, we have been taught the speech of birds, and we have been given from all things. This is indeed a clear favor " ﴿16﴾

2. Bilqis بلقيس ; the Queen of Sheba سَبَأ

3. No. Only few countries are kingdoms and are ruled by a king or queen. This is the case nowadays and in the past as well.

▬ **Verse number (3) worksheet (A)**

II. 1. The five daily prayers. Fasting Ramadan and performing Hajj.

2. Allah ﷻ and Prophet Muhammad ﷺ .

3. Prophet Muhammad ﷺ .

4. By reading and understanding the following verses from Surat al-Hashr الحَشر (59:7) and Surat al-Imran آل عِمران) 3:31)

Surat (الحَشر - 59)	Verse (7)	﴿ وَمَآ ءَاتَىٰكُمُ ٱلرَّسُولُ فَخُذُوهُ وَمَا نَهَىٰكُمْ عَنْهُ فَٱنتَهُواْ وَٱتَّقُواْ ٱللَّهَ إِنَّ ٱللَّهَ شَدِيدُ ٱلْعِقَابِ ﴾ " And Whatever the Messenger gives you, accept it, and whatever he forbids you, refrain from it. And fear Allah; indeed, Allah is severe in punishment "
Surat (آل عِمران) 3-	Verse (31)	﴿ قُلْ إِن كُنتُمْ تُحِبُّونَ ٱللَّهَ فَٱتَّبِعُونِي يُحْبِبْكُمُ ٱللَّهُ وَيَغْفِرْ لَكُمْ ذُنُوبَكُمْ وَٱللَّهُ غَفُورٌ رَّحِيمٌ ﴾ " Say, "If you love Allah then follow me; Allah will love you and forgive you your sins: for Allah is All-Forgiving, Most Merciful." "

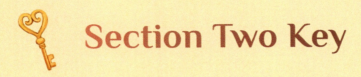

Section Two Key

- ### Verse number (4) worksheet (A)

  I. مِن شَرِّ الوَسوَاسِ الخَنَّاسِ

  II.   **1.**   شَرِّ
        2. The retreating

- ### Verse number (4) worksheet (B)

  1. From
  2. The evil of
  3. The whisperer
  4. The retreating

- ### Verse number (5) worksheet (B)

  I. الذي يوسوس في صُدُور النَّاس

  II. 1. صُدُور
       2. Whispers.

- ### Verse number (6) worksheet

  III.   From among jinn and mankind

سورَةُ النّاس

Surat An-Nas

Chapter 114

Reflection worksheets

Verse number (1) reflection worksheet (A)

I. Read the following short paragraph:

Among many mankind that Allah ﷻ Almighty has created, some are destined to become fathers, mothers, and teachers. We can call a father "Lord of the house" رَبُّ المَنْزِل because he is in charge of the household and fulfills its financial needs. The father protects the family and manages its affairs in a caring and loving way.

In the same way a mother can be called "Lady of the house" رَبَّةُ المَنْزِل because she is in charge of the internal affairs of the household and fulfils her many duties with patience, love, and care. The father and the mother can also be good teachers for the other members of the household and in this respect, they are educators; مُرَبِّي (father) and مُرَبِّية (mother). Allah is teaching us in verse one that He is the Lord of all mankind رَبُّ النَّاس. He created all of us and He is our Provider and Sustainer. He provides to the believer and the disbeliever at the same time. This is clearly stated in Surat al-Baqarah البَقَرَة (2:126)

﴿ وَإِذْ قَالَ إِبْرَٰهِـمُ رَبِّ ٱجْعَلْ هَـٰذَا بَلَدًا ءَامِنًا وَٱرْزُقْ أَهْلَهُۥ مِنَ ٱلثَّمَرَٰتِ مَنْ ءَامَنَ مِنْهُم بِٱللَّهِ وَٱلْيَوْمِ ٱلْآخِرِ قَالَ وَمَن كَفَرَ فَأُمَتِّعُهُۥ قَلِيلًا ثُمَّ أَضْطَرُّهُۥ إِلَىٰ عَذَابِ ٱلنَّارِ وَبِئْسَ ٱلْمَصِيرُ ﴾

" And [remember] when Ibrahim said, "My Lord, make this city [of Makkah] a sanctuary and provide its people with fruits — those among them who believe in Allah and the Last Day." [Allah] said, "As for those who disbelieve, I will grant them enjoyment for a short while, then I will force them into the punishment of the Fire. What a terrible destination! "

Allah is the only one that gives us life and the only one that can take it away. He is our Protector and the Manager of all of our affairs. You can also read about this meaning in Surat al-Shu'ara' الشُّعَرَاء (26: 78-81)

﴿ ٱلَّذِى خَلَقَنِى فَهُوَ يَهْدِينِ ﴿78﴾ وَٱلَّذِى هُوَ يُطْعِمُنِى وَيَسْقِينِ ﴿79﴾ وَإِذَا مَرِضْتُ فَهُوَ يَشْفِينِ ﴿80﴾ وَٱلَّذِى يُمِيتُنِى ثُمَّ يُحْيِينِ ﴾

" Who created me, so He guides me ﴿78﴾ and it is He Who provides me with food and drink ﴿79﴾ and when I am ill He heals me ﴿80﴾ and He will cause me to die and then bring me back to life ﴿81﴾ "

II. Answer the following questions:

1. Why is a father called the lord of the house رَبُّ المَنْزِل? Why is a mother called the lady of the house رَبَّةُ المَنْزِل?

   ....

   ....

2. Who is the Lord of ALL mankind رَبُّ النَّاس? ....

3. True or False:

   a) Allah provides for ALL mankind: the believers and the disbelievers.

   b) Doctors heal us and thus give us life.

   c) I should always obey my parents and elders even when they ask me to do haram such as lying or stealing.

   d) The people of the Prophet Muhammad ﷺ, Quraysh, believed that Allah ﷻ is the Lord of Kaaba اللهُ رَبُّ الكَعْبَة.

4. What would you say to someone who just lost their father or mother to make them feel better?

   ....

Verse number (1) reflection worksheet (B)

I.   Read the following short paragraph:

During our childhood we always run to our parents or elders for protection and safety when we are scared or feel threatened. As we mature and become more independent, we realize that our parents sometimes need protection themselves. We become aware of new types of evil such as the evil of the unseen. Allah ﷻ orders Prophet Muhammad ﷺ and all the Muslims to say a supplication of remembrance that would protect from evil:
" I seek refuge with the Lord of mankind ". Allah ﷻ created everything and His knowledge extends to the seen and the unseen evils that could harm us. Allah is the Lord of Power and Might as stated in Surat adh-Dhariyat الذاريَات (51:58)

> ﴿ إِنَّ ٱللَّهَ هُوَ ٱلرَّزَّاقُ ذُو ٱلْقُوَّةِ ٱلْمَتِينُ ﴾
> " Indeed, it is Allah Who is the All-Provider, Lord of Power, the Mighty "

He is our ultimate refuge and destination for safety, protection, and comfort from evil.
Our tongues should be repeating remembrance while our hearts rest assured with faith in the Lord of ALL mankind رَبُّ النَّاس.

II.   Answer the following questions:

1.   What should we do when we are fearful?

   ....

2.   Give examples of the seen and unseen evils that could harm us?

   ....

3.   True or False:

   a)   Muslims believe in the seen and the unseen creations of Allah ﷻ

   b)   Seeking refuge and doing remembrance is done by the tongue only.

   c)   Allah ﷻ is the Mighty and is the Lord of Power thus there is nothing that can defeat Him.

   d)   Once we reach adulthood, we don't need protection as our parents and elders have taught us everything.

4.   Reflect on verse number one's meaning in your own life

   ....

Verse number (2) reflection worksheet (A)

I. Read the following short paragraph:

Queen of Sheba had a great throne. She was a wise and peaceful queen. She governed her people with mutual consultation and deliberation. Her name was queen Bilqis بلقيس and Allah ﷻ had given her a great and prosperous kingdom. In spite of all these favors queen Bilqis and her people worshiped the sun instead of Allah. Satan had made their deeds appealing to them and turned them away from the right path. Allah inspired King Solomon سُلَيْمَان عَلَيْهِ السَّلَام about the right path of monotheism and Islam. When king Solomon سُلَيْمَان عَلَيْهِ السَّلَام learned from the hoopoe bird about the kingdom of Sheba and Queen Bilqis and their misguided ways, he sent them a noble letter. The letter said: It is from Solomon سُلَيْمَان عَلَيْهِ السَّلَام , "In the name of Allah, the Most Compassionate, the Most Merciful."

Do not be arrogant toward me, but come to me in full submission". Quran (27:30-31)

Queen Bilqis was wise and wanted to prevent war and bloodshed. She sent king Solomon سُلَيْمَان عَلَيْهِ السَّلَام great gifts instead. We can read about king Solomon's سُلَيْمَان عَلَيْهِ السَّلَام answer in the following verse from Surat an-Naml النَّمل (27:36)

﴿ فَلَمَّا جَاءَ سُلَيْمَٰنَ قَالَ أَتُمِدُّونَنِ بِمَالٍ فَمَا ءَاتَىٰنِ ٱللَّهُ خَيْرٌ مِّمَّا ءَاتَىٰكُم بَلْ أَنتُم بِهَدِيَّتِكُمْ تَفْرَحُونَ ﴾

◊ When the envoy came to Solomon, he said, "Do you seek to appease me with wealth? What Allah has given me is far better than what He has given you. Rather, it is you who take pleasure in gifts ◊

When queen Bilqis realized the truth about Allah (that He is the only one worthy of worship) she said: "My Lord, I have wronged myself, and now submit along with Solomon سُلَيْمَان عَلَيْهِ السَّلَام to Allah ﷻ, the Lord of the worlds" . Surat an-Naml النَّمل (27:44)

﴿ قَالَتْ رَبِّ إِنِّى ظَلَمْتُ نَفْسِى وَأَسْلَمْتُ مَعَ سُلَيْمَٰنَ لِلَّهِ رَبِّ ٱلْعَٰلَمِينَ ﴾

" She said, "My Lord, I have wronged myself, and now I submit along with Solomon to Allah, the Lord of the worlds" "

II.   Answer the following questions about the story of the Queen of Sheba   (سَبَأ)

1.   **What is the name of the Queen of Sheba ?** ....

2.   **What did Sheba prostrate to ?** ....

3.   **Is prostration an act of worship? Why ?** ....

   ....

4.   **True or False:**

   a)   King Solomon سُلَيمَان عليه was a prophet and Allah ﷻ taught him the language of the hoopoe bird.

   b)   Queen Bilqis بلقيس worshiped the sun and was too arrogant to submit to Allah ﷻ as the only Lord worthy of worship.

   c)   People should always keep their old ways and traditions in life because the forefather's way is the best way.

   d)   It is important to elect the best people for leadership because leaders are responsible for making major decisions for the whole community.

5.   **In what surah can you read about the full story of the Queen of Sheba? What are the verse numbers?**

   ....

   ....

طائر الهدهد
THE HOOPOE
BIRD

Verse number (2) reflection worksheet (B)

I. **Read the following verse from Surat aal-Imran** آل عِمْرَان **(3:26)**

﴿ قُلِ ٱللَّهُمَّ مَٰلِكَ ٱلْمُلْكِ تُؤْتِى ٱلْمُلْكَ مَن تَشَآءُ وَتَنزِعُ ٱلْمُلْكَ مِمَّن تَشَآءُ وَتُعِزُّ مَن تَشَآءُ وَتُذِلُّ مَن تَشَآءُ ۖ بِيَدِكَ ٱلْخَيْرُ ۖ إِنَّكَ عَلَىٰ كُلِّ شَىْءٍ قَدِيرٌ ﴾

" Say, "O Allah, Lord of the dominion, You give dominion to whom You will and take it away from whom You will; You honor whom You will and humiliate whom You will. All good is in Your Hand. You are Most Capable of all things "

II. **Answer the following questions:**

1. **What is the meaning of the word dominion?**

....

....

2. **Who gives and who takes away dominion?**

....

3. **True or False:**

a) We should be afraid of people of authority because they can control us.

b) Allah ﷻ is the King of ALL mankind's kings because He can give dominion and He can take it away.

c) Hard work and being smart always leads to fortune and riches in this life.

d) Whatever good happens to you is from Allah ﷻ , but whatever bad happens to you are from yourself.

4. **Decide if the following statement is correct or incorrect and then explain why. Since the power to control and govern is ultimately with Allah ﷻ only, a Muslim is not obligated to follow any man-made jurisdiction or control.**

....

....

....

Verse number (3) reflection worksheet (A)

I.   Read the following paragraph:

Prophet Muhammad ﷺ was born in the city of Makkah in the Arabian Peninsula in Asia. His tribe was called Quraysh. Quraysh were the leaders of the city of Makkah and had many noble and rich members. Quraysh's major source of wealth was trade with the northern region (Canaan Region) بِلاد الشَّام at summer time and the southern region - بِلاد اليَمَن at winter time. Another major source of wealth was the Hajj season and the trade that was built around it. The people of Makkah sold handmade statues and idols during Hajj for profit. Prostrating to statues and idol worship was common practice around the Kaaba. The people of Makkah believed in Allah as Lord of mankind, but they performed acts of worship to the statues. They argued that the idols are Allah's partners which interceded (intervened) for them. We can read about this meaning in Surat az-Zumar الزُّمَر (39:3)

﴿ أَلَا لِلَّهِ ٱلدِّينُ ٱلْخَالِصُ وَٱلَّذِينَ ٱتَّخَذُوا۟ مِن دُونِهِۦٓ أَوْلِيَآءَ مَا نَعْبُدُهُمْ إِلَّا لِيُقَرِّبُونَآ إِلَى ٱللَّهِ زُلْفَىٰٓ إِنَّ ٱللَّهَ يَحْكُمُ بَيْنَهُمْ فِى مَا هُمْ فِيهِ يَخْتَلِفُونَ إِنَّ ٱللَّهَ لَا يَهْدِى مَنْ هُوَ كَـٰذِبٌ كَفَّارٌ ﴾

﴿Indeed, sincere devotion is due to Allah alone. As for those who take others as guardians besides Him, [saying], "We only worship them so that they may bring us closer to Allah." Allah will judge between them concerning that over which they differ. Allah does not guide anyone who is a liar and a persistent disbeliever ﴾

Allah ﷻ has sent prophet Muhammad ﷺ to the people of Quraysh with the following clear messages:

Surat (آل عِمْرَان -3)	Verse (2)	﴿ ٱللَّهُ لَآ إِلَـٰهَ إِلَّا هُوَ ٱلْحَىُّ ٱلْقَيُّومُ ﴾ " Allah: None has the right to be worshiped except Him, the Ever-Living, the All-Sustaining "
Surat (الأَنْعام -6)	Verse (6)	﴿ قُلْ إِنَّ صَلَاتِى وَنُسُكِى وَمَحْيَاىَ وَمَمَاتِى لِلَّهِ رَبِّ ٱلْعَـٰلَمِينَ ﴾ " Say, "Indeed, my prayer, my sacrifice, my living and my dying are all for Allah, Lord of the worlds "

Verse number (3) reflection worksheet

II.   Answer the following questions:

1.   Where was Prophet Muhammad ﷺ born? ....

2.   What is the name of Prophet Muhammad's ﷺ tribe? ....

3.   Where did Quraysh travel to in the summer time? and in the winter time?

....

....

4.   **True or False:**

a) The people of Quraysh worshiped Allah ﷻ .

b) Idol worshipping is encouraged in Islam since idols intercede for us.

c) In Makkah, the people of Quraysh sacrificed animals as an act of devotion to their idols.

d) Idols can't help themselves and thus they can't help others.

5.   While performing the five daily prayers, in what position would a Muslim be closest to Allah ﷻ ? How do you know? ....

....

....

The Arabian Peninsula

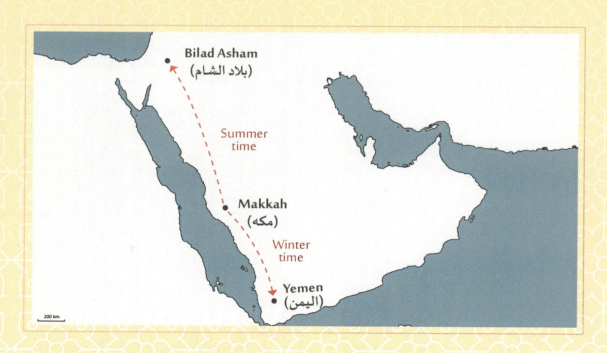

Verse number (4) reflection worksheet

I.   Read the following paragraph:

In this verse, Allah ﷻ is warning us about the evil of the retreating whisperer. The devil or Satan is the origin of ALL evil in ourselves and in this world. He makes bad actions look easy, fun, and good. He makes good deeds seem hard to accomplish, less appealing, and bad. When we remember our Lord, our Creator, and our God (Allah)ﷻ, the devil retreats. The devil never gives up and when he fails to make us do evil at one moment, he is sure to come back again with new sinful ideas. People of reflection are in a constant state of remembrance. Believers ask Allah ﷻ to protect them wherever they are and in whatever they do. We can read about these meanings in the following verses from Surat al-Mu'minun المُؤمِنُون (23-97:98)

> وَقُل رَّبِّ أَعُوذُ بِكَ مِنْ هَمَزَٰتِ ٱلشَّيَٰطِينِ ﴿97﴾ وَأَعُوذُ بِكَ رَبِّ أَن يَحْضُرُونِ ﴿98﴾
>
> And say, "My Lord, I seek refuge with You from the temptations of the devils ﴿97﴾
>
> And I seek refuge with You, my Lord, that they even come near me ﴿98﴾

The devil's ultimate goal is to keep us away from the garden of Eden جَنَّة عَدن. A place that is forbidden for the devil and his sort. We can read about this meaning in Surat al-A'raf الأَعْرَاف (7:18)

> ﴿ قَالَ ٱخْرُجْ مِنْهَا مَذْءُومًا مَّدْحُورًا ۖ لَّمَن تَبِعَكَ مِنْهُمْ لَأَمْلَأَنَّ جَهَنَّمَ مِنكُمْ أَجْمَعِينَ ﴾
>
> ﴿Allah said, "Get out of here, disgraced and expelled! I will certainly fill Hell with you and those who follow you all together ﴾

II.   Answer the following questions:

1.   According to the Quran, who is the origin of ALL evil in ourselves and in the world? ....

2.   How could we protect ourselves from the devil's whispers?
....

3.   List some types of worship that a believer does on a daily basis to protect him/her self from the evil of the retreating whisperer.
....

4.   **True or False:**
   a)   The devil constantly whispers to the disbelievers only.
   b)   Allah knows mankind and the devil best because He created everything.
   c)   If we don't see or can't touch something, then it doesn't exist.
   d)   The devil gives up when we seek refuge in Allah ﷻ

5.   What is your plan to protect yourself from the evil of the retreating whisperer?
....
....

اللَّهُ أَكْبَرُ
اللَّهُ أَكْبَرُ
حي على الصلاة

Verse number (6) reflection worksheet (A)

I.   Read the following verses from the Holy Quran about jinn.

Surat (الرَّحمن -55)	Verse (15)	﴿ وَخَلَقَ ٱلْجَآنَّ مِن مَّارِجٍ مِّن نَّارٍ ﴾ ﴿and He created the jinn from a smokeless flame of fire﴾
Surat (الجِن -72)	Verses (1-2)	قُلْ أُوحِيَ إِلَىَّ أَنَّهُ ٱسْتَمَعَ نَفَرٌ مِّنَ ٱلْجِنِّ فَقَالُوٓاْ إِنَّا سَمِعْنَا قُرْءَانًا عَجَبًا ﴿1﴾ يَهْدِىٓ إِلَى ٱلرُّشْدِ فَـَٔامَنَّا بِهِ ۖ وَلَن نُّشْرِكَ بِرَبِّنَآ أَحَدًا ﴿2﴾ " Say, "It has been revealed to me that a group of jinn listened [to the Qur'an,] and they said, 'Indeed, we have heard a wondrous recitation ﴿1﴾ that guides to the right way, so we have believed in it, and we will never associate anyone with our Lord ﴿2﴾"
Surat (الجِن -72)	Verse (14)	وَأَنَّا مِنَّا ٱلْمُسْلِمُونَ وَمِنَّا ٱلْقَـٰسِطُونَ فَمَنْ أَسْلَمَ فَأُوْلَـٰٓئِكَ تَحَرَّوْاْ رَشَدًا ﴿14﴾ " And among us are some who are Muslims and some who are deviant . Those who accepted Islam have sought the true guidance ﴿14﴾"
Surat (الكَهف -18)	Verse (50)	وَإِذْ قُلْنَا لِلْمَلَـٰٓئِكَةِ ٱسْجُدُواْ لِـَٔادَمَ فَسَجَدُوٓاْ إِلَّآ إِبْلِيسَ كَانَ مِنَ ٱلْجِنِّ فَفَسَقَ عَنْ أَمْرِ رَبِّهِ ۗ أَفَتَتَّخِذُونَهُ وَذُرِّيَّتَهُۥٓ أَوْلِيَآءَ مِن دُونِى وَهُمْ لَكُمْ عَدُوٌّۢ ۚ بِئْسَ لِلظَّـٰلِمِينَ بَدَلًا ﴿50﴾ "And [remember] when We said to the angels, "Prostrate before Adam," so they all prostrated except Iblīs, who was one of the jinn, but he disobeyed the command of his Lord. Will you then take him and his progeny as protectors instead of Me, even though they are your enemies? What a terrible exchange for the wrongdoers! ﴿50﴾"
Surat (الأعْرَاف -7)	Verse (27)	إِنَّهُۥ يَرَىٰكُمْ هُوَ وَقَبِيلُهُۥ مِنْ حَيْثُ لَا تَرَوْنَهُمْ ۗ إِنَّا جَعَلْنَا ٱلشَّيَـٰطِينَ أَوْلِيَآءَ لِلَّذِينَ لَا يُؤْمِنُونَ ﴿27﴾ "He and his offspring see you from where you cannot see them. We have made devils allies to those who disbelieve ﴿27﴾"
Surat (النِّسَاء -4)	Verse (76)	ٱلَّذِينَ ءَامَنُواْ يُقَـٰتِلُونَ فِى سَبِيلِ ٱللَّهِ ۖ وَٱلَّذِينَ كَفَرُواْ يُقَـٰتِلُونَ فِى سَبِيلِ ٱلطَّـٰغُوتِ فَقَـٰتِلُوٓاْ أَوْلِيَآءَ ٱلشَّيْطَـٰنِ ۖ إِنَّ كَيْدَ ٱلشَّيْطَـٰنِ كَانَ ضَعِيفًا ﴿76﴾ "The believers fight in the way of Allah, whereas the disbelievers fight in the way of Tāghoot. So fight the allies of Satan. Indeed, the scheme of Satan is ever weak ﴿76﴾"

Verse number (6) reflection worksheet (A)

II.   Answer the following questions:

1.   What are jinn created from? ....

2.   Who are Satan's allies? ....

3.   Is Satan a jinn? What is your proof? ....

....

4.   **True or False:**
   a) The wicked scheme of the devil is always strong.

   b) Jinn can see us, but we can't see them.

   c) All jinn are disbelievers.

   d) Satan caused our parents - Adam ﷺ and Eve عليها السلام (آدَم وَحَوَاء)

      to be expelled from the Garden

5.   What is the meaning of the word الطَّاغُوت?

....

....

Verse number (6) reflection worksheet (B)

I.   Read the following paragraph:

There are many people that we meet and interact with on a daily basis. Nowadays, technology has enabled many platforms for thousands of interactions with a limitless number of people (mankind). Allah ﷻ is clearly teaching us in this verse that some people will try to influence us to do sinful acts. Their words imitate the sinful whisper of Satan. Allah ﷻ is yet again asking us to seek refuge and stay away from their sinful whisper as well. We can read more about these meanings in the following verses :

Surat (الزُّخْرُف - 43)	Verses 67-68	ٱلْأَخِلَّآءُ يَوْمَئِذٍ بَعْضُهُمْ لِبَعْضٍ عَدُوٌّ إِلَّا ٱلْمُتَّقِينَ ﴿67﴾ يَٰعِبَادِ لَا خَوْفٌ عَلَيْكُمُ ٱلْيَوْمَ وَلَآ أَنتُمْ تَحْزَنُونَ ﴿68﴾ On that Day, close friends will become enemies to one another, except the righteous ﴿67﴾ [It will be said to them], "O My slaves, there is no fear for you Today, nor will you grieve ﴿68﴾
Surat (الكَهْف - 18)	Verse 28	وَٱصْبِرْ نَفْسَكَ مَعَ ٱلَّذِينَ يَدْعُونَ رَبَّهُم بِٱلْغَدَوٰةِ وَٱلْعَشِيِّ يُرِيدُونَ وَجْهَهُۥ وَلَا تَعْدُ عَيْنَاكَ عَنْهُمْ تُرِيدُ زِينَةَ ٱلْحَيَوٰةِ ٱلدُّنْيَاۖ وَلَا تُطِعْ مَنْ أَغْفَلْنَا قَلْبَهُۥ عَن ذِكْرِنَا وَٱتَّبَعَ هَوَىٰهُ وَكَانَ أَمْرُهُۥ فُرُطًا ﴿28﴾ Be patient with those who call upon their Lord morning and evening, seeking His pleasure. Do not turn your eyes away from them, desiring the adornments of the life of this world. And do not obey one whose heart We have made heedless of Our remembrance, who follows his desires and whose affairs [deeds] are at loss ﴿28﴾

II.   Answer the following questions:

1.   What are sources of sinful whisper in the hearts of ALL mankind?

   ....

2.   How can we protect ourselves from the harm of the retreating whisperers from among jinn and mankind? ....

   ....

3.   True or False:

   a)   Allah loves all believers in monotheism including the underprivileged.

   b)   On judgement day ALL close friends will become enemies to one another.

   c)   We should always listen to our friends' advice because they like us.

   d)   The extreme love of this world and its pleasures will help us connect to the hereafter.

4.   What is your duty towards your friends as a believer?

   ....

   ....

5.   Think about examples for adornments (زِينَة) of this world that you personally struggle with. What are the Islamic guidelines that have to be followed in matters of worldly adornments and possessions.

   ....

   ....

   ....

Verse number (6) reflection worksheet (C)

I. Keeping Good Company: Read the following Hadith:

عَن أَبِي مُوسَى الأَشعَرِي ﷺ: أَنَّ النَبِي ﷺ قَال:" إِنَّمَا مَثَلُ الجَلِيس الصَّالِح وَجَلِيس السُّوء : كَحَامِل المِسكِ، وَنَافِخ الكِيرِ، فَحَامِلُ المِسكِ إِمَّا أَن يُحْذِيَكَ، وَإِمَّا أَن تَبتَاعَ مِنهُ، وَإِمَّا أَن تَجِدَ مِنهُ رِيحاً طَيِّبةٍ، وَنَافِخُ الكِيرِ إِمَّا أَن يُحْرِقَ ثِيَابَكَ، وَإِمَّا أَن تَجِدَ مِنهُ رِيحًا مُنْتِنَةً" مُتَفَقٌ عَلَيهِ

Abu Musa Al-Ash'ari ﷺ reported that the Prophet ﷺ said:

" The example of the righteous companion and the evil companion is like that of the musk-seller and the forge blower. As for the musk-seller, he will either give you some as a present, or you will buy some from him, or you will just receive a good smell from him. Whereas the one blowing the bellows will either burn your clothes, or you will receive a nasty smell from him."

Companion Types	A	B
Example	....	....
Possible Outcomes:	....	....
Overall Outcome: (Circle one answer)	Good / Bad	Good / Bad

Verse number (1) reflection worksheet (A)

II. 1. Because they are both in charge of the household and fulfill its many duties and affairs with patience, love, and care. They both provide for the other family members to make sure that they have what they need for a happy and successful life. They also educate and lead the family members to safety.

2. Allah ﷻ

3. True or False:

a) True

b) False: Doctors heal us and save us from dying by the will (permission) of Allah only, for He is the one that gives life or takes it away. This is clearly stated in Surat ash-Shu'ara الشُّعَرَاء (26: 80)

> ﴿ وَإِذَا مَرِضْتُ فَهُوَ يَشْفِينِ ﴾ "and when I am ill He heals me"

c) False. Obedience is due to none if it contravenes the Creator's commands

لا طَاعَةَ لِمَخْلُوق فِي مَعْصِيَةِ الخَالِق

However, we should treat our parents with respect and compassion even when we might disagree with them at times for matters of belief. The Quran clearly states this fact in Surat al-Isra' الإِسْرَاء (17:24)

> ﴿ وَٱخْفِضْ لَهُمَا جَنَاحَ ٱلذُّلِّ مِنَ ٱلرَّحْمَةِ وَقُل رَّبِّ ٱرْحَمْهُمَا كَمَا رَبَّيَانِى صَغِيرًا ﴾
> "and lower to them the wing of humility out of mercy, and say, "My Lord, have mercy upon them as they raised me when I was small." "

d) True. However, they worshiped idols and statues to bring them closer to Allah which is an act that took them out of Islam and Monotheism.

دين التوحيد بالألوهية لله تعالى وَحْدَهُ

4. Allah is our Lord and He takes care of all of us. We have to accept what Allah has given us (the good and the bad) and have faith in Him carrying us through

Reflection Worksheets Key

Verse number (1) reflection worksheet (B)

II. 1. We should seek refuge with our Lord Allah ﷻ by moving our tongues with remembrance أَعوذُ بالله . Our hearts should rest assured since our Protector, Allah ﷻ, is able, with His might and power, to protect us from evil.

2. Seen evil: whisper from sinful humans asking us to perform acts that are harmful to us or to someone else. Unseen evil: the devil's sinful whisper وَسْوَسَة الشَّيطَان.

3. True or False:

    a) True

    b) False: By our tongues (saying remembrance) and by our hearts believing in the All powerful and Almighty Allah ﷻ and His ability to protect us, our loved ones, and our property.

    c) True

    d) False: Allah has created the universe and He knows about evils that we don't know about or even see. His protection and guidance are essential for our safety.

Verse number (2) reflection worksheet (A)

II. 1. Queen Bilqis بلقيس

2. The sun.

3. Yes. When people lie face down in submission to something they express complete helplessness and adoration. In Islam, all of these acts and feelings are only performed toward the one and only Lord and Creator Allah .

4. True/False:

    a) True.

    b) False.

    c) False. We have to be flexible and open-minded in order to accept the truth when it is presented to us. We can read about this meaning in Surat al-Maidah سُورَة المَائِدَة (5:104)

> ﴿ وَإِذَا قِيلَ لَهُمْ تَعَالَوْاْ إِلَىٰ مَاۤ أَنزَلَ ٱللَّهُ وَإِلَى ٱلرَّسُولِ قَالُواْ حَسْبُنَا مَا وَجَدْنَا عَلَيْهِ ءَابَاۤءَنَاۤ أَوَلَوْ كَانَ ءَابَاؤُهُمْ لَا يَعْلَمُونَ شَيْئًا وَلَا يَهْتَدُونَ ﴾
>
> " And when it is said to them, "Come to what Allah has sent down and to the Messenger," they say, "What we have found our forefathers upon is sufficient for us." Even though their forefathers knew nothing nor were they guided? "

    d) True.

5. Surat an-Naml النَّمل (27:20-44)

Reflection
Worksheets Key

— **Verse number (2) reflection worksheet (B)**

II. 1. The power to control and govern.

2. Allah ﷻ

3. True or False:

a) False. Allah ﷻ is in control of our destiny: the good and the bad. Allah is in control of people of authority as well.

b) True.

c) False. The results are always with Allah. With His permission and mercy we succeed in this life. However, we always have to work hard to achieve our goals. God will reward us for working hard even when we don't achieve our goals.

d) True. We can read this in Surat an-Nisa النِّسَاء (4:79)

﴿ مَّآ أَصَابَكَ مِنْ حَسَنَةٍ فَمِنَ ٱللَّهِ وَمَآ أَصَابَكَ مِن سَيِّئَةٍ فَمِن نَّفْسِكَ وَأَرْسَلْنَٰكَ لِلنَّاسِ رَسُولًا وَكَفَىٰ بِٱللَّهِ شَهِيدًا ﴾

"Whatever good happens to you is from Allah, but whatever bad happens to you is from yourself. We have sent you [O Prophet] as a messenger to mankind, and sufficient is Allah as a witness. "

We should stay away from sinning and Allah will protect us. Sinning can bring us a quick punishment in this world, or later punishment in the hereafter.

4. The statement is incorrect. Islam teaches us to follow and respect the laws of the land that we live in. For example, we have to follow traffic laws because they keep us safe and preserve precious human lives. They also prevent the loss of property and any other damage or harm.

— **Verse number (3) reflection worksheet**

II. 1. He was born in the city of Makkah in the Arabian Peninsula in Asia.

2. Quraysh.

3. Canaan Region بِلاد الشَّام (north); Yemen Region بِلاد اليَمَن (south).

4. True/False

a) False. The people of Quraysh worshiped idols.

b) False. Worship is only due to Allah ﷻ. We can directly call upon our Lord and God, Allah ﷻ, to heal, provide, forgive, and protect us. There is no need for anyone or anything to intervene between us and Allah.

c) True

d) True

5. The position of prostration (forehead on the ground) فِي الصَّلاة عِنْدَ السُّجُود

It was narrated by Abu Hurairah that: The Messenger of Allah said: " The closest that a person can be to his Lord, the Mighty and Sublime, is when he is prostrating, so increase in supplication then."

عَن أبِي هُرِيرة، أنَّ رَسُولَ اللهِ صَلى الله عليه وَسَلَّم قَالَ:" أقْرَب مَا يَكُونُ العَبد مِن رَبِّه عَزَّ وَجَلَّ وَهُوَ سَاجِد فَأكْثِرُوا الدُّعَاء "

Reflection Worksheets Key

Verse number (4) reflection worksheet

II.1. The devil إِبْلِيس

  2. We say: أَعُوذُ بِاللهِ مِنَ الشَّيْطَانِ الرَّجِيم and we believe Allah is Mighty and the devil's scheme is weak.

  3. By performing daily morning and evening remembrance أَذْكَار الصَّباح وَأَذْكار المَسَاء. Reading and listening to the Quran. Increasing our knowledge about what is permissible (حَلَال) and what is forbidden (حَرَام) in Islam.

  4. True/False

    a) False. No mankind can escape the constant whisper of the devil.

    b) True.

    c) False. We can't see the devil or the angels, but we believe they exist because we believe that the Quran is the truth from God (the Creator of every thing).

    d) False. The devil never gives up and will come back with new evil whispers. Constant seeking refuge is the only protection from his evil.

  5. By performing daily morning and evening remembrance أَذْكَار الصَّباح وَأَذْكار المَسَاء. Reading and listening to the Quran. Increasing our knowledge about what is permissible (حَلَال) and what is forbidden (حَرَام) in Islam.

Verse number (6) reflection worksheet (A)

II.1. A smokeless flame of fire.

  2. The disbelievers among jinn and mankind and our own evil desires هَوَى النَّفْس.

  3. Yes, Satan or the devil is a jinn. Review Surat al-Kahf الكَهْف (18:50)

  4. True/False

    a) False. The wicked scheme of the devil is always weak. Review Surat sn-Nisa النِّسَاء (4:76)

    b) True. Review Surat al-A'raf الأَعْرَاف (7:27)

    c) False. Review Surat al-Jinn الجِن (72:11,14)

    d) True.

  5. The word الطَّاغُوت means:
False objects of worship, such as devils, idols, stones, the sun, angels, saints, graves, rulers, etc.

Reflection
Worksheets Key

■ **Verse number (6) reflection worksheet (B)**

II. 1. Disbelievers, Satan, and one's own worldly desires اتِّبَاع هَوَى النَّفس

2. By performing daily morning and evening remembrance أَذْكَار الصَّبَاحِ وَأَذْكَار المَسَاء Reading and listening to the Quran. Increasing our knowledge about what is permissible (حَلَال) and what is forbidden (حَرَام) in Islam. Also, by keeping good righteous company.

3. a) True. We are counseled in the Quran to be patient with ALL people of faith (18:28).

b) False. Except the righteous.

c) False. We always have to follow the guidelines of Allah.

d) False. Quran (18:46)

> ﴿ ٱلْمَالُ وَٱلْبَنُونَ زِينَةُ ٱلْحَيَوٰةِ ٱلدُّنْيَاۖ وَٱلْبَٰقِيَٰتُ ٱلصَّٰلِحَٰتُ خَيْرٌ عِندَ رَبِّكَ ثَوَابًا وَخَيْرٌ أَمَلًا ﴾
> " Wealth and children are the adornments of the life of this world, but the lasting righteous deeds are better with your Lord in reward and better in hope. "

4. Help and remind them to do good. Love for them what we love for ourselves. Provide good advice in matters that we know about. Set a good example for them. Never lie, cheat, or disrespect them in anyway. Keep our promises to them and never make a promise that we can't keep.

> عَن أَنَس بن مَالك ﷺ خَادِم رَسُول الله ﷺ، عَن النبي ﷺ قَال
> "لا يُؤمِنُ أَحَدُكم حَتَى يُحِبَّ لِأَخِيه مَا يُحِبُّ لِنَفسِه ".
> Anas Ibn Malik reported that the Prophet said: "None of you is a real believer until he loves for his brother what he loves for himself".

5. Allah blessed us by making the majority of the adornments lawful in this world (7:32)

> ﴿ قُلْ مَنْ حَرَّمَ زِينَةَ ٱللَّهِ ٱلَّتِىٓ أَخْرَجَ لِعِبَادِهِۦ وَٱلطَّيِّبَٰتِ مِنَ ٱلرِّزْقِۚ قُلْ هِىَ لِلَّذِينَ ءَامَنُوا۟ فِى ٱلْحَيَوٰةِ ٱلدُّنْيَا خَالِصَةً يَوْمَ ٱلْقِيَٰمَةِۗ كَذَٰلِكَ نُفَصِّلُ ٱلْءَايَٰتِ لِقَوْمٍ يَعْلَمُونَ ﴾
> " Say, "Who has forbidden the adornments and lawful provisions[8] that Allah has brought forth for His slaves?" Say, "They are for the believers in the life of this world, and they will be exclusively for them on the Day of Resurrection. This is how We make the verses clear for people who have knowledge "

However, the following guidelines have to be followed:

a)   The adornments and possessions are halal in Islam to begin with

b)   They have to be obtained by halal and lawful ways

c)   They shouldn't distract from duties of worship towards Allah

Reflection
Worksheets Key

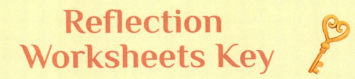

— **Verse number (6) reflection worksheet (C)**

Companion Types	A	B
Example	حَامِل المِسك musk-seller	نَافِخُ الكِير **forge blower**
Possible Outcomes:	1. Get some as a present 2. Buy some 3. Receive a good smell	1. Burnt clothes 2. Nasty smell
Overall Outcome: (Circle one answer)	(Good) / Bad	Good / (Bad)

سُورَةُ النَّاسِ

Surat An-Nas

Chapter 114

Quiz Review

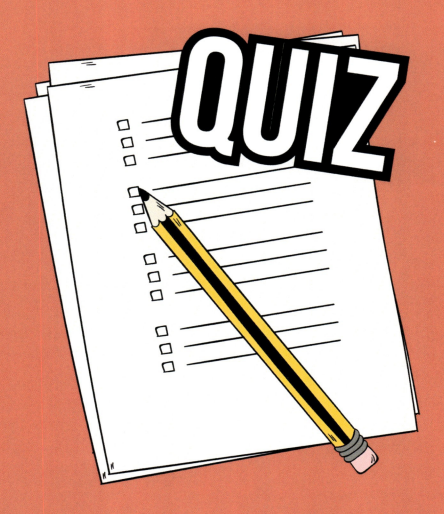

Word Search!

Find each of the words in the box below.
Words may go across, down, up, or diagonally.

قُلْ   ٱلْجِنَّةِ

أَعُوذُ   صُدُورِ   ٱلنَّاسِ

مَلِكِ   خَنَّاسِ   وَسْوَاسِ

ا	ل	أ	و	س	و	ا	س
و	ن	ع	ق	ص	أ	م	ى
م	ص	د	و	ر	ا	ق	ى
خ	ن	ا	س	ذ	خ	م	ل
ق	س	ة	ن	ج	ل	ل	ا
ص	ا	س	ن	ل	ا	ك	م

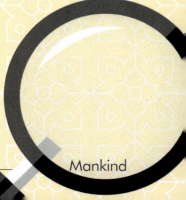

Mankind

Directions: Match the word
to its correct English meaning.

Meaning	Word
A. King	[ ] ١-خَنَّاسٍ
B. Breasts	[ ] ٢-ٱلنَّاسِ
C. God	[ ] ٣-وَسْوَاسِ
D. Evil	[A] ٤-مَلِكِ
E. Jinn	[ ] ٥-صُدُورِ
F. I seek refuge	[ ] ٦-قُلْ
G. Mankind	[ ] ٧-أَعُوذُ
H. Retreating	[ ] ٨-إِلَٰهِ
I. Whisperer	[ ] ٩-ٱلْجِنَّةِ
J. Say	[ ] ١٠-شَرِّ

Complete writing the verses below

1

قُلْ ....
....

3
.... إِلَهِ

2
مَلِكِ ....

5
.... ٱلَّذِى
....
....

4
.... مِن
....
....

6
.... مِنَ
....

CRISS-CROSS WORD PUZZLE

Use the clues found on the next page to fill in the words below. Words can go across or down. Letters are shared when the words intersect.

Mankind _____

CRISS-CROSS
WORD PUZZLE
CLUES

ACROSS

3. Head of household
8. Prophet Muhammad ﷺ (birth place)
9. To ask Allah ﷻ (for protection) - (two words)
12. Prophet and king
13. Winter travel region
14. Prophet Muhammad's ﷺ (tribe name)

DOWN

1. The One worshiped
2. The only One worthy of worship
4. All humans
5. Always comes back to whisper
6. The whisperer
7. Example of a good companion
10. Made from a smokeless flame of fire
11. Meaning of the Arabic word قُلْ

Quiz Review Key

Review worksheet (A) key

						ل	أ	ا
س	ا	و	س	و				
ى	م	أ	ص	ق	ع	ن		و
ى	ق	ا	ر	و	د	ص		م
ل	م	خ	ذ	س	ن	خ		
ا	ل	ج	ة	ن	س	أ		ق
م	ك	ا	ل	ن	ا	س		ص

Review worksheet (B) key

1:H	3:I	5:B	7:F	9:E
2: G	4:A	6:J	8:C	10:D

Review worksheet (C) key

قُلْ أَعُوذُ بِرَبِّ ٱلنَّاسِ (1) مَلِكِ ٱلنَّاسِ (2) إِلَٰهِ ٱلنَّاسِ (3)
مِن شَرِّ ٱلْوَسْوَاسِ ٱلْخَنَّاسِ (4) ٱلَّذِى يُوَسْوِسُ فِى صُدُورِ ٱلنَّاسِ (5) مِنَ ٱلْجِنَّةِ وَٱلنَّاسِ (6)

CRISS-CROSS WORD PUZZLE KEY

1 G O D

2 A L L A H

3 L O R D

4 M A K K A H

8 M A N K I N D

5 R E T R E A T I N G

9 S E E K R E F U G E

6 D E V I L

7 M U S K S E L E

10 J I N N

11 S A Y

13 Y E M E N

12 S O L O M O N

14 Q U R A Y S H

End of chapter
Self-Reflections

My favourite verse is ...... because ....

....
....
....
....

Currently, during this time in my life, I can relate to verse number ...... because ....

....
....
....
....

Verse number ..... reminds me of ....

....
....
....
....

I can implement verse number .... by doing the following ....

....
....
....
....

Chapter 114 takeaway points \ personal lessons learned ......

....
....
....
....

BOARD GAME

BOARD GAME RULES
Number of Players: 2-4

Goal
The aim of this game is to review Surat An-Nas and be the first to reach the **FINISH** point.

Materials Included:
1. Board
2. Questions
   (Cut & separate into 48 game cards)

Materials Needed:
1. Game pieces or pawns (1 per group) (can use different color buttons)
2. Six-sided Dice (1 per group)

Gameplay Instructions

I.   Cut & separate questions into 48 game cards. Place ALL cards face down on one side of the board (the cards are shuffled before the beginning of each game).

II.   Each team will roll the dice to determine the order of the game. The team with the highest number will go first (team A) and the team with the lowest number will go second (team B).

1.   **2 teams** play against each other (**A & B**)
2.   First question is read by **team B** member.
3.   Only one **team A** member answers the question (selected member rotates).
4.   If **team A** answers question correctly, they roll the dice and move the team marker accordingly.
5.   If **team A** doesn't answer question correctly, the **team A** marker stays in place and the dice is not rolled.
6.   The next question is read by **team A** member for the second round of play. If **team B** answers correctly then they roll the dice and move their marker accordingly; and if they answer incorrectly, they don't roll the dice or move their marker.
7.   Both teams take turns answering the questions and rolling the dice.
8.   Any team can take advantage of the short cuts when their marker lands on a short cut point.
9.   The game continues in the same way until the **FINISH** point is reached.
10.   The team that reaches the **FINISH** point first wins.

BOARD GAME QUESTIONS

What is the Quranic word that means Lord?

Answer: رَبّ

114

Recite the first 3 verses of Surat النَّاس

Answer: قُل ....

Recite the verse that is translated as follows: Say," I seek refuge with the Lord of mankind"

Answer: Verse (1)

What is the Quranic word that means: The King or The Sovereign?

Answer: مَلِك

What is the Quranic word that means whisperer?

Answer: الوَسوَاسِ

Give four examples of things we say as remembrance?

Answer: الحمد لله، الله أكبر، سبحان الله
استغفرالله، لا إله إلا الله

Unscramble the following words from verse 5:
النَّاس / يُوَسوِسُ / الذي / في صُدُورِ
Answer:
الذي يُوَسوِسُ في صُدُورِ النَّاس

Recite the verse that is translated as follows: " The King or Sovereign of mankind "
Answer: Verse (2)

This page is blank for the cutting activity on the opposite side

Fill in the blank:
Who whispers into the _____
of mankind.

Answer: Breasts

Recite the verse that is
translated as follows:
"From among jinn and
mankind"

Answer: Verse (6)

The Quranic word
النَّاس means
a) Hearts   b) Mankind
c) Angels   d) God

Answer: b

Unscramble the following
words from verse 4:
الخَنَّاس / مِن / الوَسوَاس / شَرِّ

Answer: من شَرِّ الوَسوَاس الخَنَّاس

Recite the last 3 verses
of Surat النَّاس

Answer: من شَرِّ ....

The Quranic word الخَنَّاسِ in
verse 4 means:
a) Whisperer   b) Hearts
c) Mankind   d) Retreating

Answer: d

The Quranic word شَرِّ in
verse 4 means:
a) Good   b) Mankind
c) Retreating   d) Harm

Answer: d

According to the Quran,
jinn is made of ....
a) Clay   b) Light
c) A smokeless flame of fire
d) b and c are the correct answers

Answer: c

What should we do
when we are fearful?
(Two things)
Answer:
1. We seek refuge by saying:
أَعُوذُ بِالله مِن ———————
2. Our hearts still assured with faith

The Quranic word أَعُوذُ in
verse one means
a) I seek refuge   b) Hearts
c) Say   d) Harm

Answer: a

This page is blank for the cutting activity on the opposite side

Example of unseen creations of Allah are:
a) Jinn
b) Angels
c) Mankind
d) a & b are correct

Answer: d

A father can be called رَبُّ المَنْزِل because he is:
a) In charge
b) A manager   c) A teacher
d) Responsible for household expenses   e) All of the above

Answer: e

True or False:
Doctors heal us and thus give us life.
Answer: False. Allah is the only one who gives life & can take it away.

The people of the Prophet (Quraysh) believed that Allah is:
a) Their Lord   b) Their God
c) The Lord of the Kaaba
d) a and c are correct

Answer: d. They worshiped idols.

True/False:
Prostration is an act of worship since people place their faces down in submission to something to express complete helplessness and adoration.

Answer: True

What did Sheba سَبَأ and their Queen prostrate to?
a) The moon   b) The sun
c) Status   d) Idols

Answer: b

The Quranic word قُلْ **in verse number one means**
a) I seek refuge   b) Hearts
c) Say   d) Harm

Answer: c

What is the name of the prophet who was also a king and could understand the language of the hoopoe bird?

Answer: King Solomon

What is the meaning of the Quranic word الجِنَّة ?

Answer: The jinn

Who is the king of ALL mankind's kings? Why?
Answer: اللهُ سُبحَانَهُ وَتَعَالى
Because He gives dominion & takes it away.

This page is blank for the cutting activity on the opposite side

Where is the city of Makkah located?

a) In Syria   b) In Yemen
c) In Africa
d) In the Arabian Peninsula in Asia

Answer:d

The Quranic word الطَّاغُوت **means false objects of worship such as: "**

a) Devils   b) Idols
c) Stones   d) Rulers
e) All of the above

Answer: e

**Fill in the blank:
Prophet Muhammad was born in the city of: ....**

Answer: Makkah

**Fill in the blank:
The people of Quraysh traded with ....in the summer time**

Answer: بِلاد الشَّام - North
(Canaan Region)

What are some outcomes of a forge blower's visit or companionship?

Answer: 1. Burnt clothes
2. Nasty smell

According to the hadith; an example of a righteous companion is: ....

Answer: Musk-seller
حَامِلُ المِسْك

List ALL sources of sinful whispers in the hearts of ALL mankind?

Answer:
1. Disbelievers among jinn and mankind
2. One's own evil desires

The devil makes good actions seem ....

a) Hard to accomplish   b) Bad
c) less appealing
d) ALL of the above

Answer: d

What is the name of the Queen of Sheba?

Answer:
Bilqis بَلْقيس

**True /False:
All jinn are disbelievers.**

Answer: False

This page is blank for the cutting activity on the opposite side

What is the Quranic word in verse three that means God?

Answer: إِلَه

In what surah can we read about the full story of the Queen of Sheba مَلِكَة سَبَأ and King Solomon?
Answer: Surat an-Naml
(27:20-44)

The devil makes bad actions seem ....

a) Easy   b) Fun

c) good   d) ALL of the above

Answer:d

Fill in the blank:
The people of Quraysh traded with
.................in the winter time
Answer: Southern region
- Yemen

What are some benefits that you can get from a musk-seller's visit or companionship?
Answer: 1. He will give you some as present 2. You will buy from him 3. You will just receive a good smell

---

According to the hadith; an example of an evil companion is: ....
Answer:
Forge blower نَافِخُ الكِير

What is the Prophet's hadith that talks about brotherly love?
Answer:
لا يُؤْمِنُ أَحَدُكُم حتى يُحِبَّ لِأَخِيهِ
مَا يُحِبُّ لِنَفْسِهِ.

What is the name of Prophet Muhammad's tribe?

Answer: Quraysh
قُرَيش

In what Surah can we learn about Queen Bilqis and her kingdom?

a) An-Naml   b) An-Naba'

c) An-Nas   d) An-Nasr

Answer: a

True /False:
Prostrating to statues and idol worshipping is common practice around the Kaaba nowadays.
Answer: False

Printed in the United States
by Baker & Taylor Publisher Services